Department of the Environment
Ancient Monuments and Historic Buildings

Hampton Court Palace

Greater London

by the late
G. H. CHETTLE   OBE, FSA

and
JOHN CHARLTON   MVO, MA, FSA

revised with additions by
JULIET ALLAN   MA
*Inspector of Ancient Monuments and
Historic Buildings*

LONDON: HER MAJESTY'S STATIONERY OFFICE

Contents

Acknowledgements

The portraits of William III (page 12), Mary II (page 12), Barbara Villiers Duchess of Cleveland (page 20), paintings by Bruegel (page 38), Mantegna (detail, page 35), and the Field of the Cloth of Gold (detail, page 39), are reproduced by Gracious Permission of Her Majesty the Queen. The Department gratefully acknowledges the following sources of illustrations: Ashmolean Museum (page 3), John Bethell Photography (pages 5, 8, 32), National Monuments Record (page 36), and National Portrait Gallery (page 10). Remaining photographs are Crown copyright from the DoE Photographic·Library.

Printed in Scotland by Her Majesty's Stationery Office at HMSO Press, Edinburgh.
Dd 717395 C1500 11/82 (200525)

ISBN 0 11 671130 2

History

Hampton Court was begun in the reign of Henry VIII by Thomas Wolsey, Archbishop of York, on the site of a small manor house which he leased from the Knights Hospitallers in 1514. In the following year Wolsey became a cardinal and Lord Chancellor of England. He was already the most powerful, and was rapidly becoming the richest, subject in the kingdom. This country house on the bank of the Thames was planned and furnished with a magnificence rivalling, if not surpassing, that of a royal palace. The Cardinal's household is said to have numbered nearly five hundred and, when a treaty between France and England was signed in 1527, the French ambassador and his entire retinue were entertained at Hampton Court at the Cardinal's expense. But his fall was near. Two years later he was stripped of all his wealth and power. In an effort to retain the King's favour, he had already presented to Henry VIII his manor of Hampton Court with its buildings and furnishings, its tapestries and its plate but, on 30 October 1529, all his lands and goods were declared forfeit to the King. Although he received a general pardon in February 1530 and retired to his Province of York, he was arrested in November for high treason, but died while he was being brought to London.

Henry VIII at once began to enlarge the house, making it one of the most splendid royal palaces in the kingdom. He brought each of his six wives in turn to Hampton Court as Queen. His children, Edward VI (who was born here), Mary I and Elizabeth I, each held court here and here James I presided over the Hampton Court Conference for the determining of things said to be 'amiss in the Church'. Its deliberations did little to set things right in the Church, but from it sprang the Authorised Version of the Bible. Charles I lived here as King, and, for a short time, as prisoner during the Civil War; after his death, when the royal possessions were sold by order of Parliament, the palace was retained for the use of the Protector, Oliver Cromwell, although its chapel was stripped of its 'popish' images and pictures, and plain glass was set in its windows. Charles II repaired the palace and began the formal landscaping of the park, but his brother James II rarely came here.

With the revolution of 1688 and the accession of William and Mary came the second great period of building at Hampton

Detail of a drawing by Antonius van den Wyngaerde showing Hampton Court from the river in 1558

Court. Although large enough, the Tudor palace was nearly two hundred years old and did not suit the taste or the convenience of the new sovereigns. Sir Christopher Wren was commissioned to plan a new palace. Many designs were made, and one scheme at least involved the destruction of the whole of the Tudor buildings except the Great Hall. Work was begun in 1689. The first or Base Court and the Clock Court were retained, but the third courtyard, round which the old royal lodgings were grouped, was demolished to make way for the present Fountain Court containing new suites of state and private apartments. The new building, of brick with Portland stone enrichments, was designed in the Baroque style of the day, and the gardens were replanned in the formal manner of France. But beautiful and dignified as Wren's building is, it is quiet, almost domestic, compared with the pomp of such a palace as Versailles.

Queen Mary died in 1694, and the plan for the complete rebuilding of the palace was abandoned. At William's death in 1702, the interior of the new building was still unfinished, so that the decoration of many

Cardinal Wolsey, from a manuscript in the Bibliotheque Municipale, Arras

of the rooms was done to suit the taste of Queen Anne and the first two Georges.

After the death of George II in 1760, the palace was never occupied by a reigning sovereign. In 1838 Queen Victoria opened the state apartments to the public.

Part of the east front of the Palace from a drawing of c1650

Description

Exterior

In earlier times Hampton Court, like many great houses near London, was approached by water. The royal barge carried the king between Greenwich, the Tower, Somerset House, Whitehall, Hampton Court and Richmond. Now, the usual approach is by road; the main entrance is through the **Trophy Gates,** built in William III's reign, with leaden trophies of arms on the outer piers, and, on the two middle ones, the lion and the unicorn supporting shields bearing the arms of George II. The gates lead into the **Outer Green Court.** On the left are the **Palace Barracks,** now converted into flats and offices for some of the palace staff; on the right is the river; ahead is the west front of the palace, separated from the Outer Green Court by a moat. Projecting wings, probably added by Henry VIII, flank the main entrance front of Wolsey's house. His **Great Gatehouse,** in the centre, was originally two storeys higher, with elaborate lead cupolas on the turrets, crowned by gilded weather-vanes. The upper storeys were taken down in 1770–72, and a hundred years later, much of the facing brickwork

The Great Gatehouse and Moat Bridge

was renewed. The moat was filled in during the second half of the seventeenth century, and the bridge, which Henry VIII built to replace an earlier one, was buried. When the moat was dug out again by the Office of Works in 1910, the bridge was found complete except for its parapets, which were renewed, together with the supporters of the royal arms, known as the **King's Beasts,** on either side. The beasts were recarved again in 1950.

Over the main gateway, below the oriel window, is a copy of the original panel carved with the royal arms of Henry VIII, and on each turret is a terracotta roundel, with a head in high relief of a Roman emperor. The oak doors with linen-folded panels are of Tudor date, but the stone

The unicorn of Jane Seymour, one of the King's Beasts on Moat Bridge

vaulting within the gateway was inserted in 1882.

The first courtyard, or **Base Court,** is little altered since it was built by Wolsey. The corridors which surround it gave access to lodgings in which members of his household or guests were accommodated. Tapestries were bought for rooms over the Great Gatehouse in 1522–23. Over the arch facing the court are the arms of Henry VIII copied from the original, and on the two outer turrets are the badges and initials of Queen Elizabeth I. On the opposite side of the courtyard is the second gate tower, known as **Anne Boleyn's Gateway,** perhaps because it was embellished by Henry VIII during the short reign of his second queen. The bell-turret above the gate-tower was added in the eighteenth century, but one of its bells dates from 1480 and must have belonged to the Knights Hospitallers whom Wolsey displaced. The clock was brought here from St James's Palace by William IV. The stone vaulting beneath the arch was renewed in 1882. Over the arch are Henry VIII's arms, and on the turrets are medallions of Roman emperors modelled in terracotta by the Italian Giovanni da Maiano for Cardinal Wolsey. Eight of these were made for Hampton Court in 1521, and for the King a similar series was made to decorate the 'Holbein' gate of Whitehall Palace. They were originally coloured and gilded.

Clock Court, the inner courtyard of Wolsey's house, has been altered at several periods. On the left or north side is Henry VIII's Great Hall; the east range was largely rebuilt in George II's reign; the colonnade on the south side is the work of Sir Christopher Wren while the west range, with Anne Boleyn's Gateway, is of Wolsey's building, as is shown by the beautifully modelled panel of the Cardinal's arms in

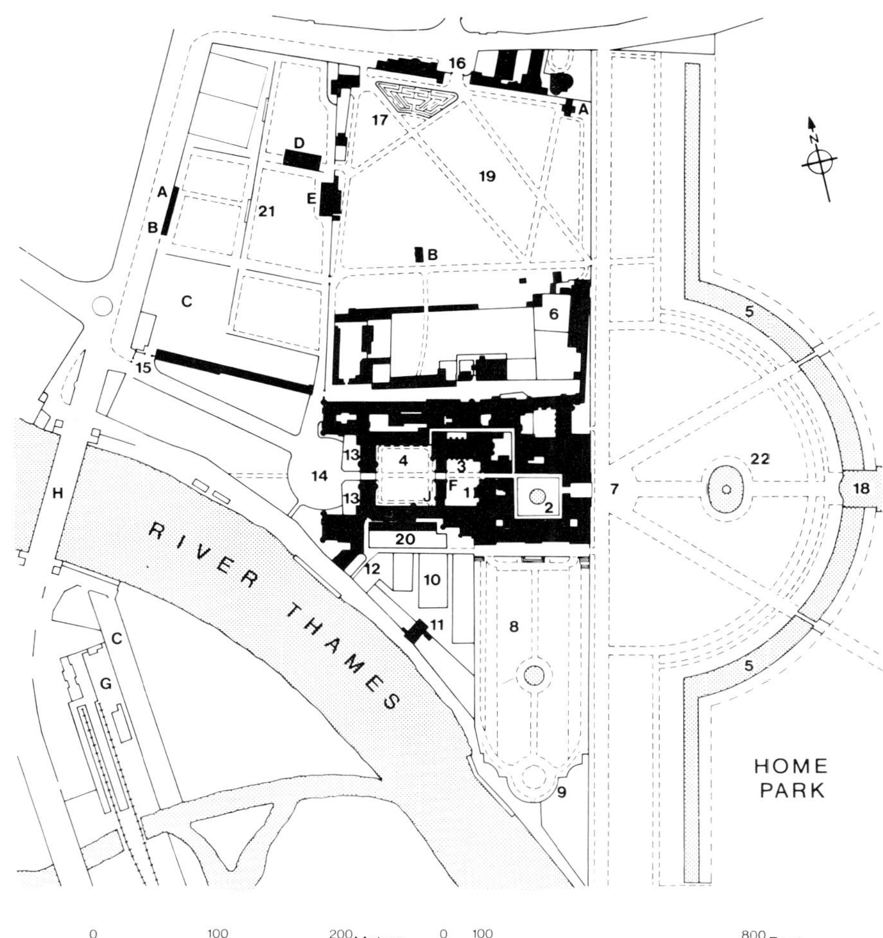

0 100 200 Metres

0 100 800 Feet

A Ladies' Lavatories
B Gentlemen's Lavatories
C Car Park
D Cafeteria
E Restaurant
F Shop
G Hampton Court Railway Station
H Hampton Court Bridge
J Ticket Office

1 Entrance to State Apartments and Renaissance
   Picture Gallery
2 Fountain Court
3 Clock Court
4 Base Court
5 Canal
6 Tennis Court
7 East Front
8 Privy Garden
9 Tijou Screen
10 Pond Garden
11 Banqueting House
12 Great Vine
13 Moat
14 West Front
15 Main Entrance (Trophy Gates)
16 Lion Gates
17 Maze
18 Long Water
19 Wilderness
20 Lower Orangery (Mantegna Gallery)
21 Tiltyard Gardens
22 Fountain Garden

Ann Boleyn's Gateway and the Great Hall from Base Court

terracotta supported by putti and sur-mounted by a cardinal's hat. The panel is of Italian workmanship, and, although the arms and hat were defaced by Henry VIII, the nineteenth-century restoration is well done. The base of the panel bears Wolsey's motto: *Dominus michi adjutor* ('The Lord is my helper'). Over the top was originally the date 1525 but this has now disappeared. Above the second-floor window is the famous **Astronomical Clock** made for the King in 1540 by Nicholas Oursian, probably to the designs of the Bavarian astronomer, Nicholas Kratzer, Fellow of Corpus Christi College, Oxford, who held the royal office of Deviser of the King's Horologies. The clock indicates the hour, the month, the day of the month, the number of days since the beginning of the year, the phases of the moon and its 'southing', from which can be calculated the approximate time of high

The Astronomical Clock

EXTERIOR

A terracotta roundel in Clock Court, depicting Julius Caesar

water at London Bridge. It will be noticed that the sun revolves around the earth, since the clock was contrived before the discoveries of Galileo and Copernicus. The dial is 7ft 10in (2.4m) in diameter, and three separate copper discs revolve at different rates round the central point, the earth.

The phases of the moon are shown; next are the names of the months, the days of the week, and the signs of the zodiac. The outer edge of this third disc is marked in 360 divisions. On the stone frame, a segmented metal ring is now mounted, bearing the hours painted in two sets of twelve; in its corners are the badges and initials of Henry VIII.

About 1840 the dial, no longer in working order, was removed to a store-room, but in 1879 it was replaced and a new mechanism was made. In 1960 it was cleaned and repainted according to the original colours revealed by cleaning. Two more of Giovanni da Maiano's terracotta roundels are set on the turrets of the gateway.

On the opposite side of the courtyard is

George II's Gateway, over which is carved the date 1732 to mark William Kent's remodelling of the range in the 'Gothick' style for George II. Further alterations were made in the nineteenth century. The gateway leads to the Fountain Court of William III's palace, and thence to the east front and the Fountain Garden. Four more roundels are set on the turrets on either side of the gate. On the right or south side of the courtyard is the Ionic colonnade which leads to the state apartments, designed by Wren for William and Mary. Just in front of the colonnade, the position of the original south range of Wolsey's courtyard is marked out in the paving. It was probably demolished when the 'Wolsey Rooms' behind the colonnade were built in the 1520s.

Visitors to the Renaissance Picture Gallery and Wolsey Rooms should enter the King's Staircase beneath the Wren colonnade and turn right. A description of the gallery will be found on page 37.

The State Apartments

Like their Tudor predecessors, William and Mary needed two sorts of accommodation: state rooms for public business, such as receiving ambassadors, holding receptions and Privy Council meetings, and conferring with ministers, and private apartments in which they could be free from some part at least of the ceremonial of the court. The state apartments occupy the first floor of Wren's building. He copied the arrangement of the demolished Tudor lodgings in placing the king's suite in the south range, overlooking the Privy Garden, and the queen's on the east side, facing the park. The queen's private apartments lie behind her state rooms, looking into Fountain Court. Because the Cartoon Gallery occupies this position on the king's side, his privy lodgings are on the ground floor (see page 29).

The state apartments were laid out in the traditional pattern determined by court etiquette. Each suite is approached by a grand staircase, leading to a guard chamber, presence chamber, privy or audience chamber, drawing room and state bedchamber, each room more exclusive than the one before. Beyond, in the south-east corner, lie the innermost closets where the two suites join, to which only the most favoured were allowed access. Behind the state apartments are back staircases communicating with the various other floors of the palace. Here were the lodgings allocated to courtiers, members of the Royal Household, and guests. The visitor views the king's apartments in the order in which the courtiers and guests of 280 years ago gained access to the king. The queen's rooms are visited in the reverse order, so that the entrance to the Queen's Audience Chamber, for example, is from

Sir Christopher Wren by Sir Godfrey Kneller

behind, instead of in front of, the Chair of State under its embroidered canopy.

The **King's Staircase,** approached from the colonnade in Clock Court, was finished and decorated about 1700. The wrought-iron balustrade was designed by the famous French smith, Jean Tijou. The walls and ceiling display an elaborate composition by the Italian painter Antonio Verrio, who died in the palace in 1707. The subject matter is complex, somewhat obscure and probably contains many features of political allegory.

The north wall, where Apollo presides over a descending sequence of figures which includes the nine Muses, Ceres, Flora, Pomona and various river-gods, may represent the benefits of the rule of William of Orange (whose orange symbol occurs elsewhere in the painting). The scenes depicted on the other (north and east) walls, however, strongly resemble incidents described in the first part of the 'Satire on the Caesars', written in Constantinople in 361 by Julian the Apostate, whose figure, writing to the instructions of Mercury, is painted on the south wall. Briefly the subject of the 'Satires' (a work not unfamiliar to late Stuart political writers) is an invitation by Romulus (here shown with the she-wolf) to the Shades of Roman Emperors to attend a banquet of the gods (who appropriately occupy the ceiling). Nemesis (with flaming sword) threatens the Emperors (or Caesars), of whom Julius is here shown out in front and Nero on the extreme right, with punishment for their misdeeds. Meanwhile, to the left, club-bearing Hercules (William III's favourite hero, whose Labours were painted by Laguerre on the north-facing elevation of Fountain Court) commends to the gods the merits of Alexander, behind whom hovers the figure of Victory. The 'Satire on the Caesars' was loudly invoked in late seventeenth-

The King's Staircase

century polemics; in this context it would be possible to regard the Emperors as representing the last of the Stuarts and Alexander as William III, the favoured of Hercules.

The staircase leads up to the **King's Guard Chamber,** the first of William III's state apartments. Here the Yeomen of the Guard stood on duty when the king was in residence. Above the panelling, the walls are lined with an elaborate display of more than three thousand arms, a form of decoration found in several of the other royal palaces, but only here still set out in the original pattern devised by William III's gunsmith, Harris.

The door opposite leads to the **King's First Presence Chamber.** (It should be noted that the name of each of the state apartments is written in gold letters above the doorway on the far side of the room). The garlands of fruit and flowers in limewood over the doors were carved by Grinling Gibbons. Facing the visitor is the Canopy of State made for William III and embroidered with his initials. Beneath it stood the Chair of State; the present chair, of the correct period, was the gift of Sir Philip Sassoon, First Commissioner of Works, in 1938. The backcloth is a modern replica to which William's original arms and motto have been applied. Opposite hangs a picture by Sir Godfrey Kneller of William III on horseback painted in 1701 for this very position. Also in their original position are the over-door paintings, two architectural fantasies by Jacques Rousseau and Achtschellincks, and, above the chimney-piece, Daniel Mytens's portrait of the second Marquis of Hamilton. The modern damask wall-hangings in this and the succeeding rooms replace tapestries removed in the nineteenth century.

The **Second Presence Chamber,** sometimes referred to in King William's time merely as the 'next room' or the 'room betwixt', has no canopy and served as an ante-room to the Audience Chamber beyond. The king sometimes dined here in public. Between the windows are pier glasses and over the chimney-piece, in its original position, is a portrait of Christian IV of Denmark, brother-in-law of James I. Above the doors are further architectural fantasies by Rousseau.

The **King's Audience or Privy Chamber** is in the centre of the south front of the Wren building, and from the windows there is a good view of the Privy Garden. The late seventeenth-century chair beneath William III's richly laced canopy replaces the original Chair of State, and was also the gift of Sir Philip Sassoon. The portrait by

Honthorst of Charles I's sister, Elizabeth of Bohemia, known as the Winter Queen, and the two beautiful pier glasses made for William III are part of the original furnishings of the room.

The **King's Drawing Room** is only partly panelled, as (like those of the three preceding rooms) its walls were originally hung with tapestries. Over the white marble chimney-piece, an overmantel with elaborate garlands, wreath and cherub heads carved by Gibbons frames a portrait of Isabella, Archduchess of Austria. The fireback shows the arms of James I.

King William III's State Bedchamber demonstrates how the decoration of the rooms became progressively richer towards the innermost of the King's apartments. The ceiling painting by Antonio Verrio shows Endymion asleep in the arms of Morpheus. Over the mantelpiece with its interesting triple mirror is Lely's portrait of Anne Hyde, Duchess of York, the mother of Queen Mary II. The red velvet state bed and matching set of chairs and stools were sold to William III by his Lord Chamberlain, the Earl of Jersey. The seventeenth-century

William III, by Sir Godfrey Kneller

Mary II, by William Wissing

Detail of the ceiling in the King's Dressing Room

close-stool, still with its original upholstery, is a rare and valuable survival. Jakob Bogdany's fine flower paintings over the doors add a further element of richness to the room. The present tapestries belong to the sixteenth-century Abraham series, of which the remainder hang in the Great Hall and Queen's Audience Chamber.

The **King's Dressing Room,** designed as the **Little Bedchamber,** also has a ceiling painted by Verrio, depicting Mars in the lap of Venus. The yellow damask bed and matching suite of furniture which made this originally one of the most sumptuous rooms in the palace have long since disappeared. From the adjoining **Writing Closet** a gib door (not open to the public) gave access to the king's stool room, further closets and the private stair which led down to his privy lodgings on the ground floor. Above the corner fireplace is a mirror in which the whole perspective of the preceding rooms is reflected. The overmantel painting of birds, and the flower pieces above the doors,

are the work of Bogdany and form part of the original decoration of the room. These small intimate rooms form a junction with the queen's suite which faces east over the Fountain Garden. The little room at the corner of the south and east fronts is known as **Queen Mary's Closet** (although never used by her) because the wall was formerly hung with needlework done by her and the ladies of her court. Only the monarch's most intimate friends and advisers would penetrate as far as these rooms.

Because Queen Mary died before the building was completed, the east side of the palace was fitted out and furnished only in the succeeding reigns.

The **Queen's Gallery,** a splendid room with a cornice carved by Grinling Gibbons and a beautiful marble chimney-piece by John Nost, was completed for William III after Mary's death. The tapestries, woven in Brussels to Gobelin designs made in 1662 by Charles Le Brun, depict the history of Alexander the Great. They are said to have been introduced by George I. The splendid blue-and-white china vases, used for displaying tulips and hyacinths, were made for William and Mary and bear their arms and cipher and the motto of the House of Nassau, *Je maintiendray*.

The **Queen's Bedchamber** was decorated in 1715 for the Prince and Princess of Wales, later George II and Queen Caroline. Sir James Thornhill's ceiling painting depicts Leucothoë restraining Apollo from entering his chariot. On its deep cove are medallion portraits of George I, the Prince and Princess of Wales, and their son Prince Frederick. The state bed, chairs and stools were made in 1715–16 for the Prince and Princess of Wales; only the bed now retains its original crimson damask upholstery.

The **Queen's Drawing Room,** in the centre of the east front, was decorated by Verrio for Queen Anne between 1703 and 1705. On the ceiling the Queen is represented as Justice. On the west wall, opposite the windows, the Queen receives the homage of the four quarters of the globe; on the north wall her husband, Prince George of Denmark, Lord Admiral of England, points to the British fleet, and on the south wall Cupid is drawn by sea-horses over the waves, while the fleet rides at anchor in the background. These paintings were covered up in 1737 and not brought to light again until 1899.

The view of the garden from the centre window is one of the finest surviving examples of formal Baroque planning in England. From this point, three avenues radiate to intersect a vast semi-circle of trees and water, and stretch on across the Home Park. Beyond the semi-circle, the middle avenue encloses the Long Water, created in the reign of Charles II but incorporated in the late seventeenth-century layout.

Detail of the state bed in the Queen's Bedchamber

The **Queen's Audience or Privy Chamber** was fitted out during the reign of George I for the Prince and Princess of Wales. The tapestries which at that time decorated the walls have disappeared; one of the series of sixteenth-century Flemish tapestries illustrating the story of Abraham, of which the remainder hang in the Great Hall and the King's Bedchamber, is now to be found here. Those seeking audience entered by the north door, facing the Chairs of State under their richly upholstered canopy. The door in the corner (not open to the public) leads to a private staircase and to the privy lodgings facing Fountain Court.

The **Public Dining Room** received its name in the reign of George II, who sometimes dined here in public, but it was originally planned as a Music or Dancing Room some 13 feet (4m) longer. It was decorated by Sir John Vanbrugh *c*1716–18 for the use of George II and Queen Caroline when Prince and Princess of Wales. In the pediment of the marble chimney-piece are the arms of George I, carved by Grinling Gibbons, who was also responsible for the rich bracketed cornice.

North of the Public Dining Room is the **Prince of Wales's Suite,** originally intended for the Princess, later Queen, Anne. Largely the work of Vanbrugh, it too was used by George II and Queen Caroline when Prince and Princess of Wales, and later by Frederick Prince of Wales and his wife, Princess Augusta, the parents of George III. The massive marble chimney-pieces in these rooms are characteristic of Vanbrugh and distinguish his work from that of Wren.

The first room is the **Presence Chamber,** now unfortunately missing its green damask Canopy of State. The **Drawing Room** facing east and north gives an unexpected view of the sheltered corner still known as Lady Mornington's Garden from that famous countess, the Duke of Wellington's mother, whose private refuge it was. With the aid of the original bills, the room has been redecorated to show how it was furnished for Frederick, Prince of Wales, in 1731. The tapestry is one of a set illustrating the Acts of the Apostles, woven at Mortlake in the seventeenth century from Raphael's famous cartoons; it depicts the Conversion of St Paul. The **Prince of Wales's Bedchamber** now contains a bed designed for Queen Charlotte *c*1775–78, possibly for the Queen's Bedchamber at Windsor Castle.

On leaving the Prince of Wales's suite, the visitor enters a small corridor. The main tour of the state apartments continues to the left (see Lobby below). To the right lie the **Princesses' Lodgings** (not normally open to the public) which were redecorated in 1978 to house some of the pictures not displayed in the state apartments. The main rooms lie within what was originally Henry VIII's Close Tennis Court, converted in the 1670s to provide lodgings for James II and his wife, when Duke and Duchess of York. Much of the panelling dates from this period when it was grained to resemble walnut. In 1717, the rooms were refurnished to accommodate the three young daughters of the Prince and Princess of Wales. The present colour scheme is loosely based on the decorative scheme of the early 1730s when the apartment was remodelled for the grown-up princesses after their parents had become king and queen.

Giving access to the Prince of Wales's staircase is a small **Lobby** containing Leonard Knyff's magnificent bird's-eye view of the Palace. It was painted *c*1700 and shows the layout of the gardens at the time. The landing overlooking the **Prince of Wales's Staircase** was built in 1717 to allow the Prince and Princess of Wales to visit their young daughters more easily. The charming balcony outside the door of the Presence Chamber should be noticed, with its elaborate wrought-iron festoons below the landing. On the walls are several pieces of Mortlake tapestry from a set depicting the inconclusive battle of 1672 between the English and Dutch fleets off Solebay on the Suffolk coast. The designs, generally attributed to William van der Velde, were woven by Francis Poyntz, who signs them with the arms of the City of London, a variant of the Mortlake shield he adopted. Among the colours flown by the English fleet appears the old version of the Union flag.

A small lobby, known as the **Ante-Room**

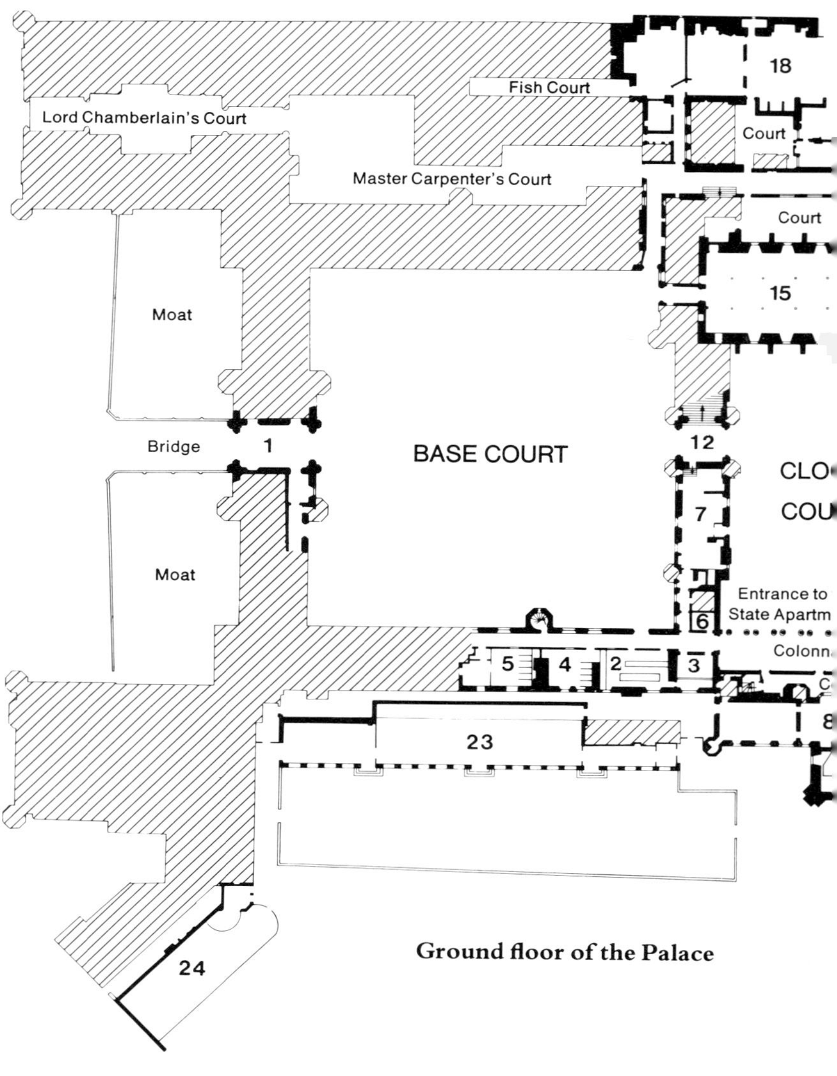

1 Great Gatehouse
2 Ticket Office
3 Cloakroom
4 Gentlemen
5 Ladies
6 Disabled WC

7 Shop
8 Exhibition
9 King's Staircase
10 Stone Hall
11 Beauty Staircase
12 Anne Boleyn's Gateway

   PLAN OF GROUND FLOOR APARTMENTS

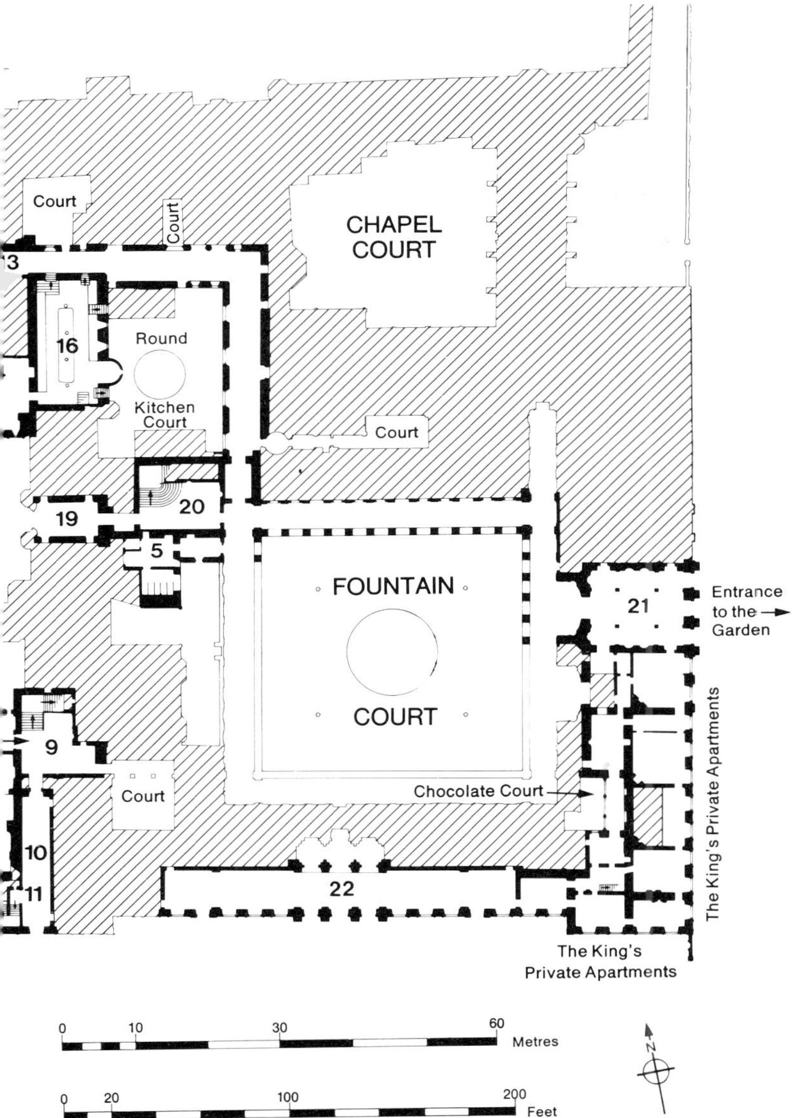

13 North Cloister
14 Privy Buttery or Beer Cellar
15 Great Buttery or Beer Cellar
16 Wine Cellar
17 Serving Place
18 Great Kitchens

19 George II's Gateway
20 Queen's Staircase
21 Pillared Vestibule
22 Upper Orangery
23 Lower Orangery (Mantegna Gallery)
24 Great Vine

PLAN OF GROUND FLOOR APARTMENTS   HAMPTON COURT PALACE 17

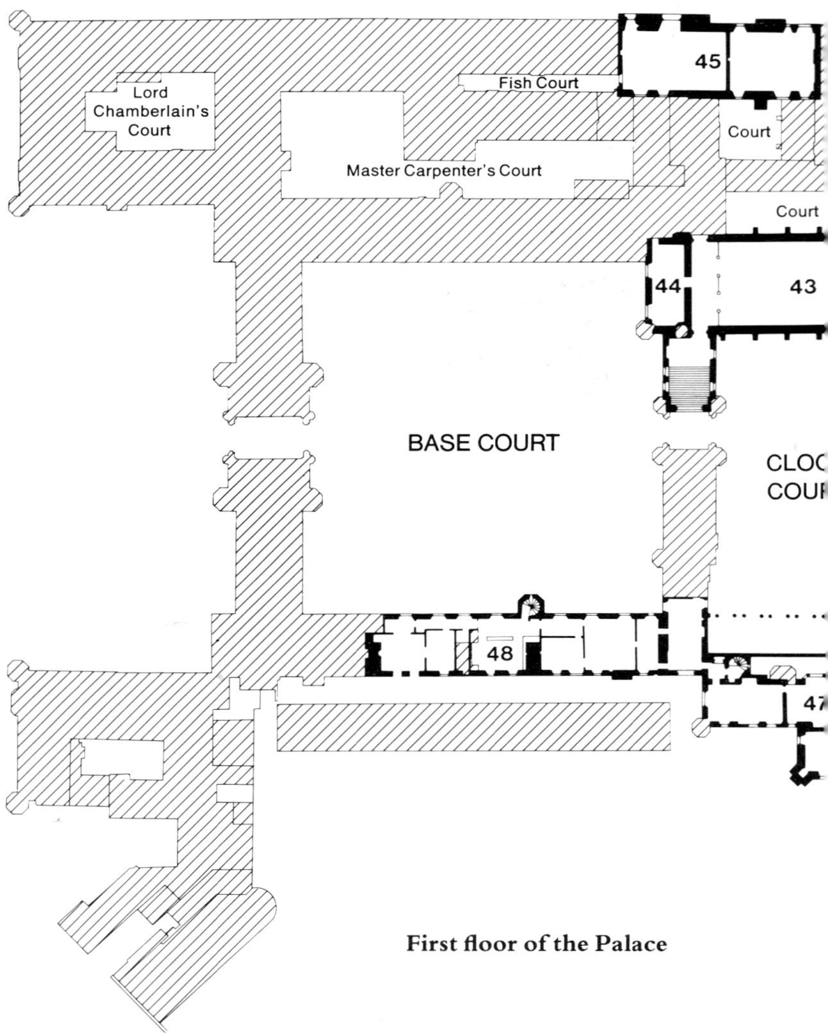

First floor of the Palace

<table>
<tr><td>

1 King's Staircase
2 King's Guard Chamber
3 King's First Presence Chamber
4 Second Presence Chamber
5 King's Audience or Privy Chamber
6 King's Drawing Room
7 King William III's State Bedchamber
8 King's Dressing Room
9 King's Writing Closet
10 Queen Mary's Closet
11 Queen's Gallery
12 Queen's Bedchamber

</td><td>

13 Queen's Drawing Room
14 Queen's Audience or Privy Room
15 Public Drawing Room
16 Prince of Wales's Presence Chamber
17 Prince of Wales's Drawing Room
18 Prince of Wales's Bedchamber
19 Lobby
20 Prince of Wales's Staircase
21 Ante Room
22 Queen's Private Chapel
23 Queen's Bathing Closet
24 Private Dining Room

</td></tr>
</table>

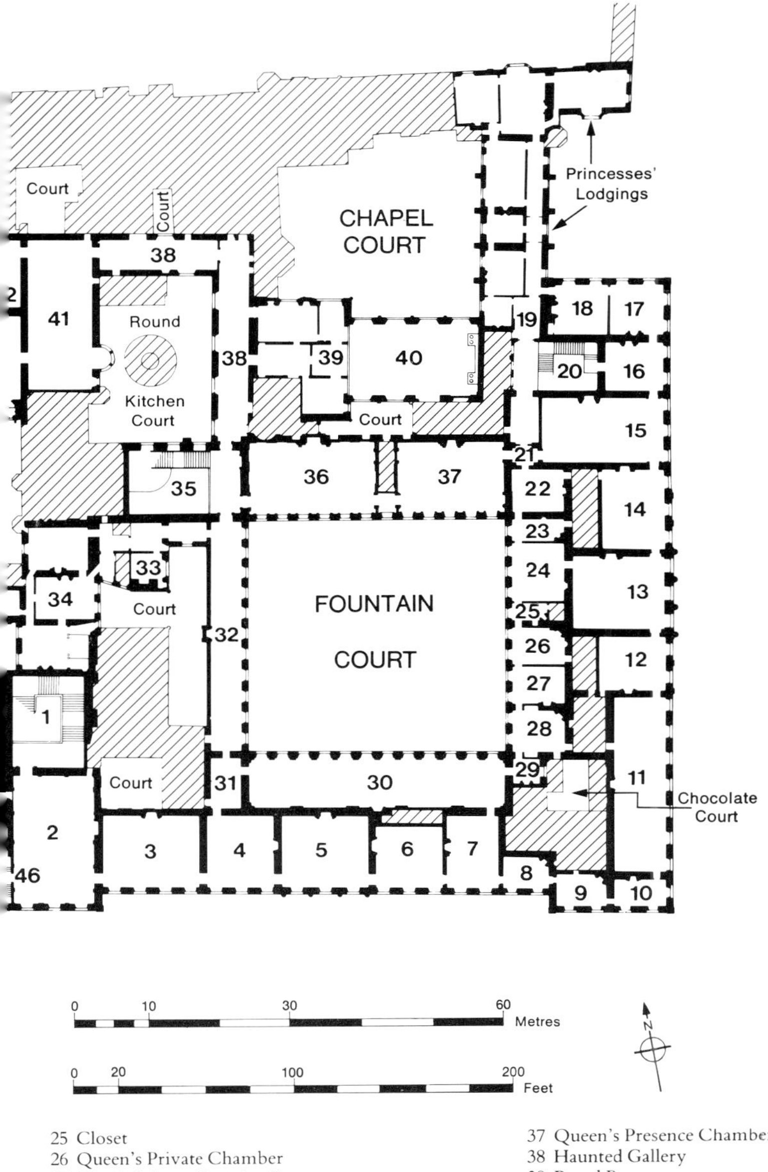

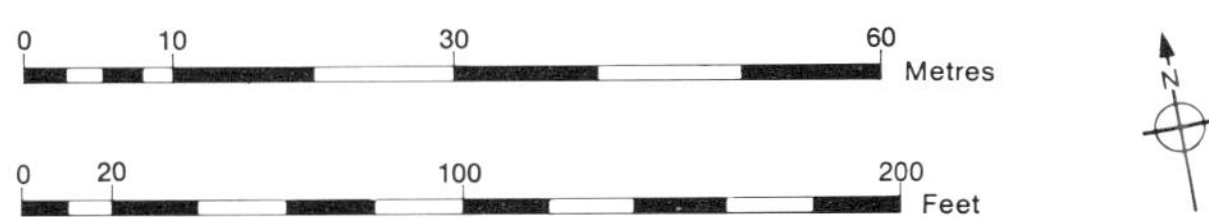

25 Closet
26 Queen's Private Chamber
27 King's Private Dressing Room
28 George II's Private Chamber
29 Lobby
30 Cartoon Gallery
31 Ante Room
32 Communication Gallery
33 Wolsey's Closet
34 Cumberland Suite
35 Queen's Staircase
36 Queen's Guard Chamber

37 Queen's Presence Chamber
38 Haunted Gallery
39 Royal Pew
40 Chapel Royal
41 Great Watching Chamber
42 Horn Room
43 Great Hall
44 Servery
45 Upper Part of Great Kitchens
46 Beauty Staircase
47 Wolsey Rooms
48 Renaissance Picture Gallery

PLAN OF FIRST FLOOR APARTMENTS   HAMPTON COURT PALACE 19 connects the Public Dining Room on the left with the Queen's Presence Chamber and Guard Chamber (described on page 21) to the right. Ahead is the suite of small oak-panelled rooms, facing into Fountain Court, originally intended as Queen Mary's private lodgings. They were later used by George II and Queen Caroline.

The **Queen's Private Chapel** or Oratory was completed for Queen Caroline in 1728. Here her chaplain read prayers while the Queen dressed in the adjoining closet.

The **Queen's Bathing Closet** has a tall marble-lined recess with basin and tap. Above the corner fireplace are shelves designed to display part of Queen Mary's collection of china.

The next room is the **Private Dining Room.** From 1795 to 1802 this and the adjoining rooms were occupied by the Stadtholder of the Netherlands, who had fled from his own country in the face of a French invasion.

A second **Closet,** with a water closet opening off it, leads to the **Queen's Private Chamber** in which is another marble basin. Beyond is the **King's Private Dressing Room** with an elaborately carved overmantel and containing a small early eighteenth-century bed hung with crimson damask. The flock wallpaper in **George II's Private Chamber** dates from about 1730 and is one of the rare examples of the period to survive. The pattern used here was a popular one and is still produced today.

A small domed **Lobby** communicates with the **Cartoon Gallery,** a splendid room occupying the whole south side of Fountain Court. Finished in 1699, it was designed by Wren to display seven of the ten cartoons painted by Raphael in 1515–16 for Pope Leo X as designs for tapestries, illustrating the lives of St Peter and St Paul, for the Sistine Chapel in the Vatican. These seven cartoons were bought by Charles I when still Prince of Wales in 1623 and were among the greatest treasures in his collection. After his execution, when Parliament ordered the sale of all the properties of 'the late Charles Stuart', these and the equally famous and valuable 'Triumph of Julius Caesar' by Mantegna were not sold. The cartoons are now in the Victoria and Albert Museum. In 1905, Baron Emile d'Erlanger gave the Crown a set of nine seventeenth-century tapestries copied from the original cartoons and seven of these now hang in this gallery. The chimney-piece, of coloured marble, has a panel below the mantel-shelf carved by John Nost, and above are two large garlands of fruit and flowers by Grinling Gibbons.

At the end of the Cartoon Gallery is an **Ante-Room** which communicates on the left with the King's Second Presence Chamber. To the right, occupying the west side of Fountain Court, lies the **Communica-**

Barbara Villiers, Duchess of Cleveland, by Sir Peter Lely

THE STATE APARTMENTS

tion Gallery, so-called because it links the king's and the queen's state apartments. On the wall are now hung the 'Windsor Beauties' painted by Sir Peter Lely and formerly at Windsor Castle. They are portraits of the ladies of Charles II's court, and include the likenesses of many well-known Restoration beauties.

At the end of the gallery, a door on the left leads through two small lobbies to a little room in the Tudor part of the palace. It is known as **Wolsey's Closet,** and is the only room which gives some idea of the decoration and colour lavished on the interior of Wolsey's palace. The lower part of the walls is lined with late nineteenth-century linen-fold panelling. Above this are set panels of the sixteenth century, representing scenes from the Passion of Our Lord. The panels had evidently been brought from elsewhere, because restoration has shown them to have been painted over work of the previous century. The ceiling is a chequer-work of richly coloured badges and ornaments with Tudor roses, Prince of Wales's feathers and rosettes, filled in with gilded Renaissance motifs. The frieze is decorated with Tudor badges, mermaids, dolphins and vases, and below, Wolsey's motto *Dominus Michi Adjutor* is repeated again and again.

Beyond the closet is the **Cumberland Suite** which takes its name from George II's son, the infamous 'Butcher' Cumberland of Culloden, who occupied it for a short time. This part of the palace was almost completely rebuilt in 1732. In an attempt to harmonise the new work with the old, the architect, William Kent, employed his own distinctive version of the Gothic style. Inside, an apartment consisting of two large state rooms, a state bedchamber and a small closet was created for the use of George II's

family. The elaborate plaster ceilings, particularly the one in the 'Gothick' manner in the last room, the handsome marble chimney-pieces and the bed alcove, with its columned screen, in the bedchamber are typical of Kent's work.

The door at the north end of the Communication Gallery opens on to the landing of the **Queen's Staircase,** with its beautiful balustrade of wrought-iron designed by Jean Tijou and its walls and ceiling painted by Kent in 1735. On the west wall, facing the first-floor landing, is a great allegorical painting by Honthorst which is signed and dated 1628. The subject is Apollo presenting the Liberal Sciences to Jupiter and Juno. The artist has depicted Charles I and his Queen as Jupiter and Juno, attended by the Countess of Carlisle and other ladies of the Court. The Duke of Buckingham represents Apollo. The lantern was made by Benjamin Goodison in 1731.

This was the ceremonial approach to the queen's state apartments. From it are entered, first the **Queen's Guard Chamber** and then, following the usual sequence, her **Presence Chamber.** The decoration of these rooms dates from the early years of George I's reign when the apartments left unfinished at the death of Queen Mary were completed for the use of the Prince and Princess of Wales. The hand of the architect Sir John Vanbrugh is evident in the boldly modelled ceiling of the Presence Chamber and in the two monumental chimney-pieces; Grinling Gibbons was responsible for much of the carving. The Guard Chamber and Presence Chamber were used again by Caroline as Queen in the 1730s; from the Presence Chamber courtiers attending her receptions or 'drawing rooms' would have passed through the Public Dining Room, which served as a large antechamber, and the Queen's Audience or Privy Chamber to the magnificent Queen's Drawing Room in the centre of the east front. The bed and accompanying suite of furniture now displayed in the Presence Chamber were made for Queen Anne's state apartments at Windsor in 1714.

Retracing his steps to the Queen's Staircase, the visitor now leaves the new building designed by Wren and enters the Tudor part of the palace.

The **Haunted Gallery** was built by Wolsey to provide access to the Chapel from his state apartments but owes its name to the story of the ghost of Catherine Howard, Henry VIII's fifth wife. Only fifteen months after her marriage, she had been accused of misconduct and arrested. According to the story, before Catherine was sent to the Tower, she was confined to her chambers in Hampton Court. She escaped, and ran along this corridor in the hope of speaking to the King, who was then hearing Mass in the Chapel Royal. Just as she reached the door of the Royal Closet, she was seized by the guard who dragged her screaming back along the gallery while the King, who must have heard her, continued his devotions. It is said that the despairing ghost of the Queen still shrieks along the gallery but no one today seems to have heard her. The gallery was redecorated in the eighteenth century. Its windows look out on to one of the smaller courtyards, known as Round Kitchen Court. On the walls are tapestries which probably came from the collection of Queen Elizabeth I. A door on the right leads to the gallery at the west end of the Chapel Royal where, in the sixteenth century, the king and queen sat in two special pews or **Holyday Closets** to hear the services; following the normal practice in

The vaulted ceiling of the Chapel Royal

a great house, the household occupied the floor of the chapel below. The much-restored Tudor ceiling of one of the Holyday closets can still be seen. The **Royal Pew** and its adjoining closets were redecorated by Sir Christopher Wren for Queen Anne in 1711. Panelling was put up and the ceiling painted by Thornhill.

The **Chapel Royal** was built by Wolsey but lavishly embellished by Henry VIII in 1535–36, when the magnificent vaulted ceiling, with its carved and gilded pendants, was constructed. The vaulting looks like stone but is in fact timber. The rest of the decoration, including the wall-painting by Thornhill and the huge oak reredos carved by Grinling Gibbons, belong to the refitting of the chapel carried out by Wren for Queen Anne. In the 1840s, the ceiling was redecorated with the advice of Pugin who seems to have been responsible for the addition of the gold stars. The windows, altered by Wren in the eighteenth century, were replaced in their original form in 1894. Only in the *trompe l'oeil* window on the far right painted by Thornhill in 1711 is the form of the eighteenth-century windows now preserved.

The Haunted Gallery continues along the north side of Round Kitchen Court to the **Great Watching Chamber,** a splendid room created by Henry VIII in 1535–36 as the Guard Chamber at the entrance to his Presence Chamber and state apartments beyond. These were destroyed by Kent in 1732, but the Great Watching Chamber shows the scale of Henry's building. Its restored ceiling is composed of intersecting ribs which curve down to form pendants, the spaces between set with roundels displaying the arms and badges of Henry VIII and Jane Seymour. The many lights of the curved bay window are filled with stained

glass designed by Thomas Willement in 1841 and containing the arms and badges of Henry VIII and Wolsey. The panels depicting Henry VIII's coat-of-arms flanked by his two supporters, the lion and the dragon, are closely based on the original Tudor heraldic glass, of which small fragments survive elsewhere. The tapestries with which this room is hung were woven in Flanders. Four of them, representing the conflict of the Virtues and the Vices, date from about 1500 and were perhaps some of those bought by Wolsey in 1522. Three depict episodes from Petrarch's Triumphs: that of Death over Chastity, Fame over Death and Time over Fame.

The next room is known as the **Horn Room.** In the early nineteenth century, it was shut up and a wide opening with double doors, possibly replacing an original Tudor doorway, was made in the wall between

Chimney stacks in Lord Chamberlain's Court

The hammer-beam roof of the Great Hall

  THE STATE APARTMENTS

the Great Watching Chamber and the Great Hall. The Horn Room is properly the serving place for the upper or dais end of the hall, and the stairs give direct access to the Great Kitchens and the cellars on the ground floor. The original oak steps survive, although the balustrade is Victorian.

The **Great Hall,** built by Henry VIII to replace Wolsey's earlier hall, was begun in 1532 and finished some four years later. So impatient was the king that the work was carried on not only in daylight but by candlelight as well. The hall is over 100ft (30m) long and 60ft (18m) high and its hammer-beam roof, enriched in every part with moulding, tracery or carving, has a span of some 40ft (12m). Amidst the carved foliage of the main supports of the roof are the royal arms, sometimes impaling those of Anne Boleyn. The elaborate pendants, in the form of richly decorated lanterns, were carved by Richard Rydge of London and show the growing influence of the Italian Renaissance. Again the badges and initials of Anne Boleyn can be seen, but before the hall was complete she had been beheaded and one of her ladies-in-waiting, Jane Seymour, was queen in her stead.

The dais, raised one step above the floor of the main hall, is lighted by a bay window with a beautiful fan vault of stone with carved pendants. The doorway leading into the Great Watching Chamber is a plaster copy of the sixteenth-century Horn Room door and was introduced in the early nineteenth century. It was on the dais that the 'high table' for senior members of the Household was set while the rest of the company sat at the common tables ranged down each side of the body of the hall. There was an open hearth in the middle of the floor near the dais; the smoke found its way up into the roof and out of an elaborate louvre, now removed. The stained glass is all Victorian, designed by Willement, and shows not only the arms, mottoes and badges of Henry VIII but also those of Wolsey, and the names and pedigrees of Henry VIII's wives, all of whom traced their descent from Edward I. The tapestries representing the story of Abraham were woven in Flanders about 1540, probably to designs by Bernard van Orley.

An oak screen at the lower end of the hall supports a minstrels' gallery. Beneath the gallery is the screens passage; to the right a flight of stairs leads down to the Great Kitchens, while on the left a wide stone staircase forms the approach to the hall from Anne Boleyn's Gateway between Base Court and Clock Court. The stone doorway in the centre leads to a small room which probably acted as a servery.

Kitchens and Offices

Beyond the Great Hall, along the north side of the palace, lay the kitchens and service quarters grouped round a series of small irregular courts. To feed not only the king himself and his guests but also the vast army of courtiers, officials, servants and hangers-on which made up the Royal Household was an enormous task requiring a whole range of kitchens and offices each with its own special function. These included a pastry and confectionery, a saucery, spicery, boiling-house and acatry as well as various larders including a fish larder, and sculleries. Above or adjacent were lodgings for the staff.

To reach the kitchens, the visitor should turn right at the foot of the stairs beneath Anne Boleyn's Gateway and then right again along the eastern side of Base Court. Under an archway in the north-east corner of the

The Tudor Wine Cellar

court is the entrance to the King's Buttery or Beer Cellar, beneath the Great Hall. A narrow cobbled passage leads to the North Cloister. On the left is **Master Carpenter's Court** (not open to the public), known in the seventeenth century as Pastry Yard and typical of the small domestic courts in this part of the palace.

The **North Cloister,** a wide dark passage, was the main traffic route for those carrying food and drink to the Great Hall and royal apartments above. The second door on the right leads to what was probably the **Privy Buttery or Beer Cellar** entered by a stone doorway with Wolsey's arms in the spandrels. Immediately inside on the right is the back door to the **King's Great Buttery or Beer Cellar** (not open to the public). In Tudor times, every member of the king's household was entitled to a daily ration of beer or wine. The beer was brewed on the premises, the wine imported. Stout oak posts support the floor of the Great Hall above the two cellars, while in the middle of the wall dividing them can be seen the stone pier which carried the central hearth above.

Beyond the Privy Buttery is the **King's Wine Cellar** underneath the Great Watching Chamber. Its fine brick vault, here rendered to look like stone, is almost identical to that of Henry VIII's wine cellar in Whitehall. Some modern wine casks have been set up on the old brick stillages to show the original arrangement.

At the far end are steps which lead back up to the North Cloister. A few paces to the left is the door at the foot of the stairs leading to the Horn Room, the serving place both for the high table in the Great Hall and for the king's apartments beyond, of which only the first, the Great Watching Chamber, now survives. Further on, on the right, two arches open into a wide **Serving Place** where, on the left-hand side, serving hatches with moulded oak frames and hinged shutters communicate with the Great Kitchen. When the food was ready, it was passed through the hatches to those waiting to carry it up the stairs to the Horn Room.

A narrow Tudor doorway gives access, via two small ancillary rooms each with an original serving hatch, to the **Great Kitchens.** Despite later alterations, they are almost certainly the finest surviving Tudor kitchens in the country. Following normal medieval practice, all the cooking was done over open fires in the huge open fireplaces which line the walls. The great height of the kitchens was probably an attempt to reduce the smoke, heat and smell created by spit-roasting over open fires. Of the original sixteenth-century roof only the two end-trusses remain, but the stone corbels which supported it can still be seen; the present roof dates from about 1840. The joist holes and other timber slots left exposed in the walls mark the position of former floors and partitions. Timber lofts may have been an original feature of the kitchens, serving either as storage space for food and equipment or as sleeping quarters for the scullion boys. By the early eighteenth century, a complex arrangement of such lofts or intermediate floors, reached by wooden stairs, seems to have existed. The remaining joist holes indicate subdivisions of the kitchens to create storage and even living accommodation after they fell into disuse in the middle of the eighteenth century.

The kitchens are now divided into three sections. The eastern section, entered first, is the oldest and was almost certainly built by Wolsey. On the right are the hatches communicating with the serving place. The large fireplace in the north wall was reduced in width shortly after it was built; in the eighteenth century, a smaller fireplace and a row of brick ovens were constructed inside it. To its right is a blocked Tudor archway, altered in the eighteenth century to give access to a now-demolished kitchen annex. On the left is the door to a little storeroom. Most of the cooking utensils on display date from the eighteenth century.

Henry VIII greatly enlarged Wolsey's kitchen. Two narrow doorways and a wide brick arch lead through into the new kitchen built for the King in 1529; since the seventeenth century, it has been divided into two parts by a half-height partition wall. The eastern section contains one of Henry's three great open fireplaces; the brick oven and smaller fireplace built inside it are seventeenth and eighteenth-century modifications. Also dating from the seventeenth century is the row of brick stewing-stoves against the partition wall.

The other half of Henry's kitchen is reached through a door at the left-hand end of the partition. The new kitchen was clearly designed to serve the common tables in the main body of the Great Hall. Two large stone hatches in its south wall, quite different in character from those in Wolsey's kitchen, opened into a second serving place. From here the food was carried across the north

The Great Kitchens

cloister and up the stairs leading into the screens passage at the lower end of the hall. Alterations made towards the end of the seventeenth century, when a doorway was cut through one of the hatches and the serving place was partitioned to form several small rooms, have partly obscured the original arrangement.

Henry's new kitchen was not built in isolation. A doorway in the west wall leads out into **Fish Court** (not open to the public), one of the small service courts around which a whole range of new subsidiary kitchens and offices, with lodging above, were grouped. Through this door, raw food or food prepared or partly prepared elsewhere must have entered the Great Kitchens. Fish Court was largely refaced in the nineteenth century.

The Tudor kitchens continued in use until the palace was abandoned by the king in the middle of the eighteenth century. In the nineteenth century, a three-storey grace-and-favour apartment, incorporating the earlier timber lofts, was constructed within the western half of Henry VIII's kitchen. This was demolished in 1978 but some of its fittings have been retained. They include an early twentieth-century range with water boiler, built into one of the original Tudor fireplaces, and a kitchen dresser and table. Traces of the demolished floors, staircases, fireplaces and partitions can be seen on the walls. The fragmentary timber floor revealed during the demolition of the old apartment may be the remains of a seventeenth-century kitchen loft. In the corner of the Tudor fireplace in the west wall of the kitchen is a partly destroyed bread oven, probably of the same date.

The visitor leaves the kitchens through the mutilated second serving hatch in the

Fountain Court

KITCHENS AND OFFICES

south wall. On the left-hand side of the passage is the original wall of the Tudor serving place containing two low-level timber hatches. Its other wall, also with a timber hatch, can be glimpsed through the door of a later room on the right. A few places further on is a narrow passage leading to what may have been the Saucery.

If the visitor turns left along the north cloister on leaving the kitchens, he will pass the foot of the stairs leading up to the screens passage at the lower end of the Great Hall. At the far end of the cloister is a third serving place, much altered in the nineteenth century, which gave access to the Privy Kitchen built for Queen Elizabeth I (not open to the public). Further on, a narrow doorway affords a glimpse of Chapel Court, beyond which is the door to the Chapel Royal flanked by carved and painted stone panels displaying the royal arms of Henry VIII and the same arms impaling Seymour, with angels supporting the crown above each shield.

A little vestibule leads into the cloisters surrounding Wren's **Fountain Court,** on the site of Henry VIII's Cloister Green Court. The court is still grassed and in the middle is a fountain in a shallow basin. Above the arches of the cloisters are the tall windows of the state apartments. The white Portland stone makes a beautiful contrast with the red brickwork, and the carved wreaths in the form of lion-skins surrounding the circular windows of the second storey add richness to the design. On the south side these wreaths frame twelve panels depicting the Labours of Hercules, painted by Louis Laguerre.

From the east cloister walk, a semi-circular bay opens into a pillared vestibule leading to the Fountain Garden on the east front. A description of the gardens begins on page 30. Those wishing to visit the king's private apartments first should enter by the door in the south-east corner of the vestibule.

The King's Private Apartments

The **King's Private Apartments** on the ground floor were reached from the state apartments above by a small private staircase. Very little is known about how they were furnished or used in King William's day, only that they seem to have included an eating room and drawing room, now the Large and Small Oak Rooms (not open to the public) at the far end of the Upper Orangery, and several closets. A special kitchen catered for William's passion for

View of the Wren building from the gardens

chocolate; 'his breakfast', a contemporary tells us, 'was only a dish of chocolate without any water in it'.

George II made greater use of the private apartments than William III had done, a reflection of the increasing relaxation of court life during the first half of the eighteenth century. Altered in the nineteenth century, when they were occupied by a series of grace-and-favour residents, the rooms have been redecorated to display pictures from the Royal Collection. Three small closets have been partially furnished to give some idea of what they may have looked like during King William's lifetime. One room contains a collection of historic prints and engravings of the palace and gardens bequeathed by Ernest Law (1854–1930). Law, who lived much of his life as a grace-and-favour resident at Hampton Court, is chiefly remembered for his monumental three-volume history of the palace. From the king's private apartments, the visitor re-enters the pillared vestibule.

The Gardens

Wren's building was conceived not in isolation but the centrepiece of a vast formal landscape in which buildings and gardens were carefully integrated to form a unified whole. Despite some later modifications, much of the late seventeenth-century garden layout survives remarkably intact and provides a rare opportunity to appreciate the scale and magnificence of Baroque planning.

A bird's-eye view of Hampton Court c1700 by Johannes Kip

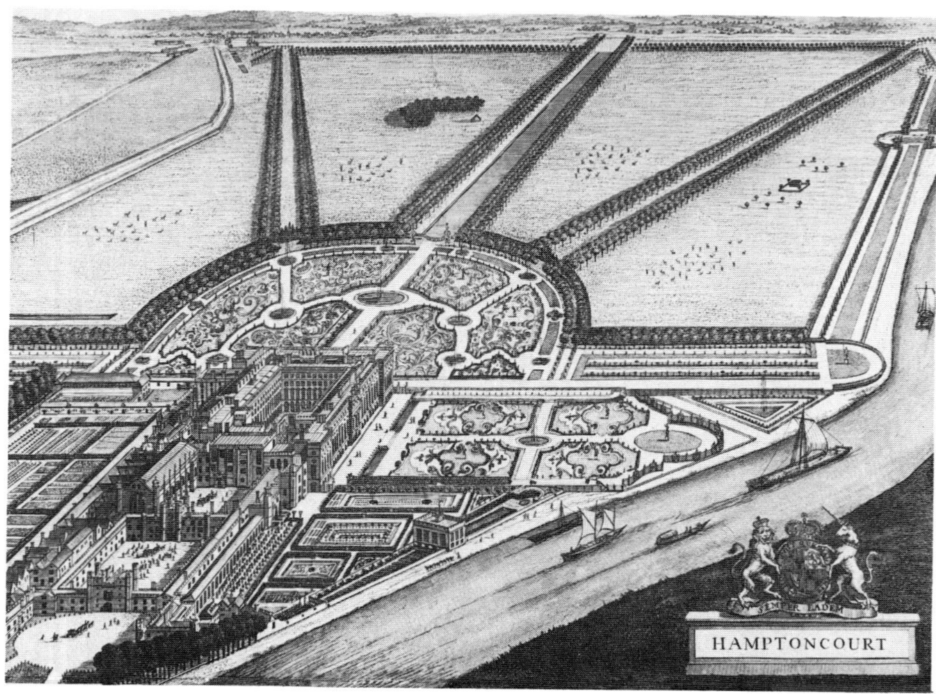

The East Front

Decorative carving on the centre-piece of the East Front

From the pillared vestibule which lies on the central axis of Wren's most important vista, three openings, containing highly decorative wrought-iron screens by Jean Tijou, lead out on to the **Broad Walk.** This wide gravel terrace, laid out in 1700, stretches from the Flower Pot Gate on the Kingston Road to the River Thames, a distance of nearly half a mile.

The principal elements in the design of the **Fountain Garden**—the **Long Water** and the three great lime **Avenues** radiating in a *patte d'oie* to form a double semi-circle of trees—date from Charles II's reign. The influence of André le Nôtre, Louis XIV's garden designer at Versailles, whom Charles II invited to England in 1662, is evident although the *patte d'oie* is more characteristic of his compatriot André Mollet. Wren's new building, begun in 1689, was carefully aligned to fit the existing layout, although the opportunity was taken to enlarge and embellish it. Within the great semi-circle, another Frenchman, Daniel Marot, designed an elaborate parterre with dwarf box hedges cut in scrolly patterns, statues and fountains. Fine wrought-iron gates made by Tijou are still in position at the entrance to the lime avenues.

Further alterations to the gardens were made by Queen Anne (1702–14) and her successors. The Queen, who reputedly disliked the smell of box, had the parterre swept away in favour of wide lawns, while beyond the semi-circle of limes, an enclosing canal was built. Since then, the lines of the original layout have been blurred but not totally obscured by the passage of time and by changes in fashion. The present statues all date from the nineteenth century when the original ones were removed to Windsor by George IV.

The Palace from the Pond Garden

From the Fountain Garden, there is a fine view of Wren's building. It has a rectangular block-like quality which contrasts sharply with the picturesque turrets, gables and chimneys of the Tudor palace and relies for much of its architectural effect on the repetition of basic units, in particular windows, across wide elevations. The pattern of the windows is a vital element in the design; the variety of their shape and size reflects the internal planning of the palace, the large sash windows on the first floor lighting the state apartments and the smaller ones above, the lodgings for members of the Court. The great stone centrepiece emphasises architecturally the focal point of Wren's whole composition. Corinthian columns flank the three full length windows of the Queen's Drawing Room and support a giant pediment containing Caius Gabriel Cibber's splendid relief of Hercules triumphing over Envy. The centrepiece is further enriched with delicately carved vases of fruit and flowers and over the middle window is a symbolic composition of trumpets, sceptres and crown, with the cipher of William and Mary.

A gateway with handsome stone piers leads to the terrace on the south front of the Wren building where shallow steps descend to the **Privy Garden,** laid out in 1701 as an elaborate parterre. The original layout has now almost totally disappeared as a result of later romantic planting and natural growth. Along the east side is a raised terrace which overlooks both the Privy Garden and the Broad Walk. On the opposite side, also raised above the garden level, is an alley of hornbeam known as **Queen Mary's Bower.** At the far end, where the garden is bounded by the Barge Walk and the River, is the **Tijou Screen,** a magnificent set of twelve wrought iron gates or panels orig-inally designed for the Fountain Garden but moved to its present position in 1701.

The south front of the Wren building, like the east front, has a centre-piece of Portland stone, but it is less elaborate. Over the central window is a fine trophy of arms and above is a Latin inscription recording the building of the palace by William and Mary: GULIELMUS ET MARIA R(EX) R(EGINA) F(ECERUNT).

Until the early nineteenth century, four

A late seventeenth-century sundial in the Privy Garden

A panel from the Tijou screen in the Privy Garden

statues stood on the parapet, of which the lead figures of Mars and Hercules, now flanking the entrance to the Upper Orangery, are survivors. The blind circular windows on either side of the centrepiece originally contained paintings representing the Four Seasons by Louis Laguerre. The coats-of-arms supported by cherubs were carved by Gabriel Cibber.

The ground floor of the south range contains the **Upper Orangery.** Here orange trees planted in tubs were kept during the cold months and moved on to the terrace in summer.

At the west end of the terrace another gateway, by the foot of the steps leading to Queen Mary's Bower, opens on to a walk bounded on the left by small formal gardens enclosed by brick walls; although sometimes called the **Tudor Gardens,** they were completely replanned in the eighteenth century and again more recently. Immediately on the right, in the angle formed by the junction of the Tudor building with William III's palace, is the tiny **Knot Garden** designed and planted in 1924 to illustrate the type of garden fashionable at the end of the sixteenth century. The initials ER and the date 1568 on the stonework of the bay window overlooking this garden commemorate its reconstruction by Queen Elizabeth I. To the left are the windows of the Wolsey Rooms; the octagonal angle turret is capped by a restored lead cupola.

On the opposite side of the garden overlooking the Thames is the **Banqueting House** created for William III out of a Tudor garden tower in 1700. Approached from a raised terrace, it contains a great room overlooking the river, a panelled ante-room and two closets. Verrio's decoration of the great room, with allegorical figures of the arts on the ceiling and the loves of Jupiter on the walls, makes it one of the most important Baroque interiors at Hampton Court.

Further on, partly hiding the back of the south range of Base Court, is another orangery, built in 1701, and known today as the **Lower Orangery.** It has been con-

A detail from The Triumph of Caesar *by Andrea Mantegna*

verted into a gallery to exhibit Andrea Mantegna's celebrated cartoons of the *Triumph of Caesar* purchased for the Royal Collection by Charles I and now one of its most valuable possessions.

Close to the Lower Orangery is the **Vinery** housing the Great Vine planted in 1768.

If the visitor returns to the Broad Walk and continues beyond the East Front, he will pass first **Henry VIII's Close Tennis Court,** a tall Tudor building with buttresses, remodelled in the late seventeenth century, which is partly hidden by a garden wall. Further on is the present **Royal Tennis Court** built in the 1620s probably on the site of an earlier open court; it was substantially altered by Charles II and is still in use.

Through a gateway in the high brick wall, the visitor enters the **Wilderness** created by William III's royal gardeners in the 1690s; of the original layout only the paths and the famous **Maze** now survive. A diagonal path on the right leads to the **Lion Gate** begun in Queen Anne's reign and completed by George I. Directly opposite in Bushy Park is the famous **Chestnut Avenue** aligned on the Great Hall and intended by Wren to form the second great axial approach to his new palace. Fanelli's **Diana Fountain,** substantially remodelled, was moved from the Privy Garden to its present position in the centre of the Great Basin in 1713.

West of the Wilderness lie the **Tiltyard Gardens** on the site of the Tiltyard where tournaments were held in Henry VIII's day. An area of seven acres (2.8ha) enclosed by

Visiting the Great Vine in 1840

high brick walls provided the jousting place and contained five elaborate viewing towers for spectators. In William III's reign the Tiltyard was turned into kitchen gardens and four of the five towers were demolished, but in 1924 the remaining tower was converted into a tea-house with lawns, trees and flower beds in front; a rose garden was planted and the rest of the ground used for tennis courts, a car park, a restaurant and a cafeteria.

The Renaissance Picture Gallery and Wolsey Rooms

From the King's staircase (described on page 10), a paved passage known as the **Stone Hall** and containing classical busts gives access to the terrace overlooking the Privy garden. To the left are the private apartments (see page 29 above) designed by Wren for William III. A doorway on the right, embellished with a carved female head, opens into the **Beauty Staircase** so-called because it led from the state apartments above to William's private dining room on the ground floor (not open to the public) where the pictures by Sir Godfrey Kneller, known as the 'Hampton Court Beauties', were hung. It is a good piece of Wren design and typical of the subsidiary staircases in the palace.

A door at the top of the stairs leads back into the Tudor part of the palace. The **first two rooms** were refitted in the eighteenth century and have been altered again more recently. They are at present hung with the fine and well-preserved 'Barberini' tapestries formerly at Buckingham Palace. Of seventeenth-century north Italian needle-work, the tapestries depict, somewhat after the manner of Poussin, such scriptural scenes as the Flight into Egypt and Adoration of the Magi. Beyond are the so-called **Wolsey Rooms** which may have been used by the Cardinal himself or perhaps by guests or senior members of his household. The two smaller rooms to the right, originally one but divided in the seventeenth century, are lined with sixteenth-century linen-fold panelling, partly reset. On the right at the top of the steps in the corner of the second room is the fragment of a Tudor doorway which gave access to a stair turret destroyed by Wren's new building. The central room has plainer rather later panelling, some of it introduced as recently as 1914. Its elaborate ribbed ceiling with early Renaissance decorative motifs has been restored. The last room in the sequence also has a restored sixteenth-century ceiling incorporating Wolsey's badges, but alterations were made to the windows in the eighteenth century. From it, there is a fine view of the gardens. Much of the panelling and also the 'Arts and Crafts' style grates and door handles in this and the previous room date from 1914 when the Wolsey Rooms were occupied as a grace-and-favour apartment.

A small **lobby** links the Wolsey Rooms with the south-east corner of Base Court, the first floor of which is now occupied by the Renaissance Picture Gallery. To the right is a Tudor spiral staircase with a fine oak hand-rail while in the sides of the recess opposite can be seen the jambs of a mutilated sixteenth-century window. The **Renaissance Picture Gallery** is entered through a restored Tudor doorway to the left.

Base Court was designed to provide lodgings for guests and members of Wolsey's household. These normally consisted of one or two rooms plus a garderobe and opened off long corridors which overlooked the courtyard at ground and first-floor levels. The rooms have undergone many alterations since the sixteenth century and seem to have been largely refitted around 1700 as part of the modernisation of the palace carried out by Wren for William and Mary. From the eighteenth century until *c*1950, the rooms now comprising the Renaissance Picture Gallery were occupied as grace-and-favour apartments. Their conversion into an air-conditioned gallery for the display of pictures painted on wood was completed in 1982.

The first-floor rooms in the south-east corner of Base Court were unusually grand and may have been designed to accommodate an important member of the Court. The **first room** is more of a gallery than a chamber and the removal of later partitions has allowed its original spaciousness to be once more appreciated. It was lit by two three-light windows in the east wall, wholly or partly blocked when Wren's colonnade

was built, and by a large south-facing window which must originally have given a delightful view over the gardens to the river. The timber partition contains a Tudor door-frame revealed during building work and now restored. Beneath the later floor, a considerable quantity of rush matting, probably of seventeenth-century date was discovered; similar to that seen in paintings of the period, it accords well with the comment of a visitor to the palace in 1613 that the floors of all the lodgings and galleries were fitted with plaited matting.

To the left of the opening leading into the **second room** is the fragment of a Tudor doorway. Archaeological investigations have shown that this area originally contained two spiral staircases. By the middle of the sixteenth century, these had probably disappeared in a major replanning of this

The Massacre of the Innocents, by Pieter Bruegel the Elder

Henry VIII and Cardinal Wolsey, in a detail from The Field of the Cloth of Gold *(artist unknown)*

part of Base Court which involved raising the roof and produced an uncommonly grand suite of rooms. Rooms 2 and 3 formed a single large chamber until the insertion of the present partition around 1700. The panelling in **Rooms 3 and 4** also dates from this period although it was partly removed in the nineteenth century when hangings were introduced. The chimney-piece in the third room which replaces a Tudor one may have been moved to its present position in the centre of the south wall at the same time; the Victorian grate has been brought from elsewhere in the palace. The lincrusta paper on the ceiling is a survivor from grace-and-favour days. The present colour scheme in rooms 3 and 4 is based on decoration which existed elsewhere in the palace in the eighteenth century. The **fifth room** retains its late seventeenth-century panelling almost intact and here many layers of later paint have been removed to reveal its original graining. Graining was much employed at Hampton Court around 1700—only the royal apartments had oak panelling—and

was intended to disguise cheap pine as a more expensive wood such as walnut.

A badly damaged sixteenth-century doorway, discovered behind the panelling during conversion work, leads into a wholly new area created within the existing building to provide additional space for the display of pictures. From it are entered the so-called **Victorian Rooms.** The corridor dates from the nineteenth century when the rooms formed part of a grace-and-favour apartment, although it echoes the rather wider gallery which originally surrounded Base Court. A fragment of the sixteenth-century corridor partition survives behind later plaster at the far end. Opening off the corridor are two rooms which retain some of their Victorian fittings and which have been decorated and furnished in the style of the 1840s.

Retracing their steps along the corridor, visitors leave the gallery through a door on the left. A spiral staircase which may be an Elizabethan addition to Base Court returns them to the ground floor.

Glossary

ACATRY	Department supplying meat and fish.
CLOISTER	Covered walkway around a courtyard.
CLOSE STOOL	Chamber-pot, often of pewter, enclosed in an upholstered box.
CORBEL	A projecting stone or piece of timber used as a support.
CORNICE	The horizontal moulding projecting at top of a classical entablature.
COVE	Curved part at the edge of a ceiling, immediately above a cornice.
CUPOLA	Small domed roof, often crowning a turret.
FESTOON	Carved garland of flowers and fruit suspended from both ends.
GARLAND	A hanging cluster of fruit and flowers.
GIB DOOR	A concealed door.
GOTHIC	Style of architecture prevalent in western Europe from the twelfth to the sixteenth centuries, of which ribbed vaulting and the pointed arch are the chief characteristics.
'GOTHICK'	Term used to describe the decorative style characterised by the fanciful use of medieval gothic motifs, created by William Kent and others in the eighteenth century.
ORIEL WINDOW	Originally any large bay window. Now generally used only of a window projecting from an upper storey.
PARTERRE	A formal garden, usually adjacent to a house, composed of beds and gravel paths arranged in ornamental patterns.
PATTE D'OIE	Literally 'a goose's foot'; trees planted in a formal pattern consisting of three avenues radiating from a semi-circle.
PENDANT	A hanging ornament much used in late Gothic architecture.
PIER GLASS	A mirror hung between windows.
PUTTI	Figures of naked children or cherubs.
REREDOS	Decorated screen or wall behind an altar.
SPANDREL	The triangular space above the shoulder of an arch.
TERRACOTTA	Fired but unglazed clay of fine quality used to produce moulded ornament.
TROMPE L'OEIL	Literally 'deceives the eye'; painted decoration which creates the illusion of reality to the spectator.
VAULT	An arched ceiling of brick or stone, sometimes imitated in wood or plaster.